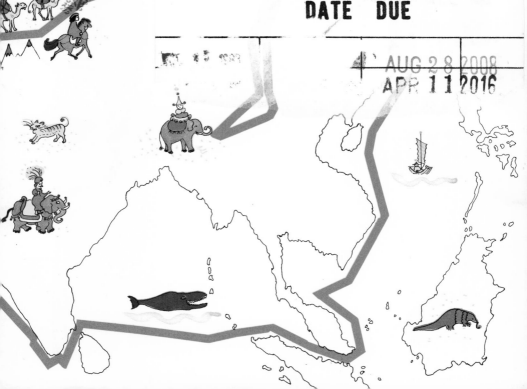

The Adventures of Marco Polo
by Demi

Holt, Rinehart and Winston · New York

Library of Congress Cataloging in Publication Data
Demi.
The Adventures of Marco Polo.
    Summary: A biography of the thirteenth-century
Venetian merchant and traveler who spent twenty-five years
in Asia and became the friend of Kublai Khan.
    1. Polo, Marco, 1254–1323?—Juvenile literature.
2. Explorers—Italy—Biography—Juvenile literature.
[1. Polo, Marco, 1254–1323? 2. Explorers.
3. Asia—Description and travel] I. Title.
G370.P9D45   950'.2'0924 [B] [92]   81-13216
ISBN 0–03–061263–2   AACR2

Per allo spirito avventuroso di
Auro Roselli

Emperor Kublai Khan of China was fascinated by the religions of the world. When the Italian explorers Nicolo and Mafeo Polo came to China, Kublai asked them to bring him holy oil from Jerusalem. They did, but first they went back to Italy to get Nicolo's seventeen-year-old son, Marco. Marco Polo sailed from Venice for the port of Acre in 1271.

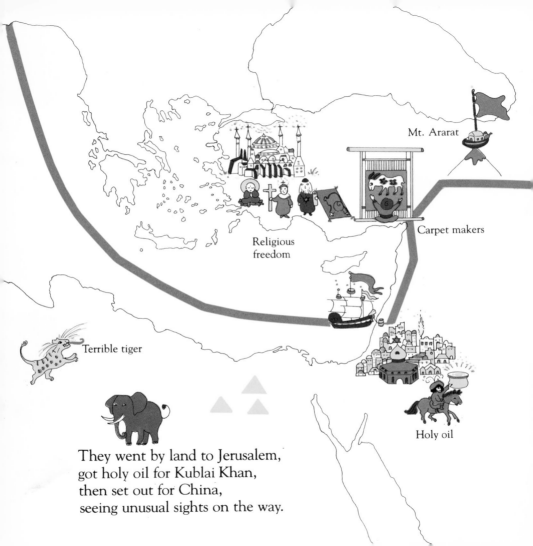

Mt. Ararat

Carpet makers

Religious
freedom

Terrible tiger

Holy oil

They went by land to Jerusalem,
got holy oil for Kublai Khan,
then set out for China,
seeing unusual sights on the way.

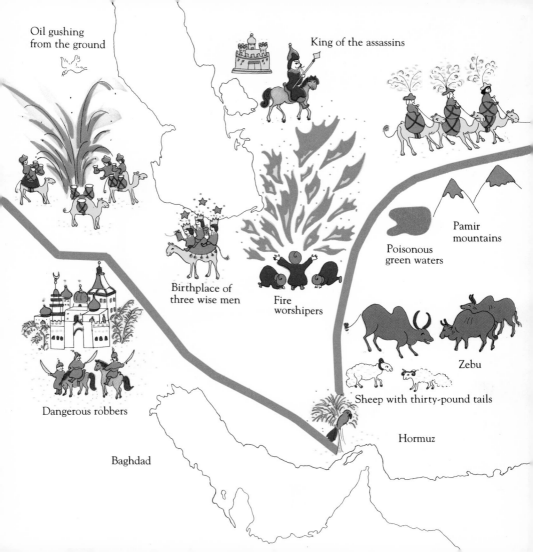

Oil gushing from the ground

King of the assassins

Pamir mountains

Poisonous green waters

Birthplace of three wise men

Fire worshipers

Zebu

Dangerous robbers

Sheep with thirty-pound tails

Hormuz

Baghdad

Marco's caravan was often plagued by

robber tribes that attacked travelers.

But, finally, he arrived in Hormuz, which was so hot
that people spent the day in water up to their chins.

Later, Marco had to fight fierce winds that blew the sand into whirling columns.

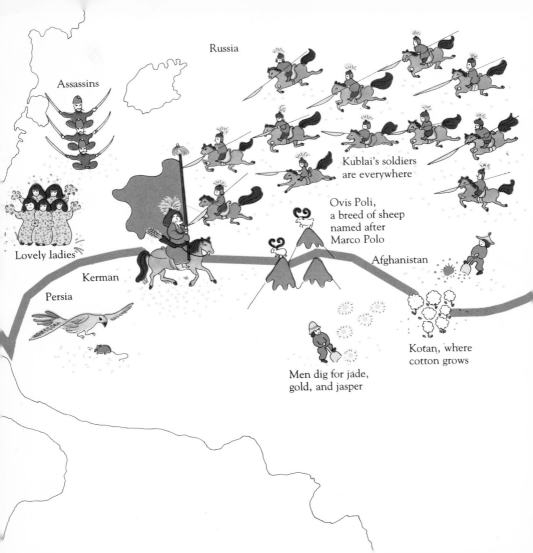

Russia

Assassins

Lovely ladies

Kerman

Persia

Kublai's soldiers
are everywhere

Ovis Poli,
a breed of sheep
named after
Marco Polo

Afghanistan

Kotan, where
cotton grows

Men dig for jade,
gold, and jasper

Outer Mongolia

Kublai's palace

Asbestos
is invented

Buddhists

Peking

Gobi Desert

Yaks

Heat waves

Singing sands

Bleached bones of travelers
who didn't make it

China

At last, he arrived in Kerman, and followed
the silk route to China.
The emperor awaited him at the other end.

Marco arrived with the holy oil for the great Kublai Khan.

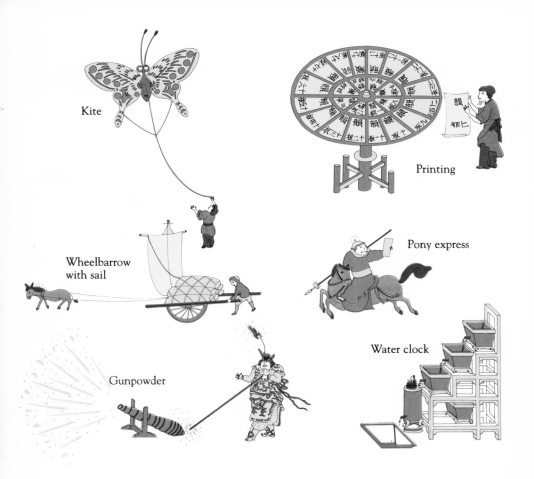

Kite

Printing

Wheelbarrow with sail

Pony express

Gunpowder

Water clock

Marco saw remarkable Chinese inventions.

Umbrella

Compass

Spaghetti

Spinning wheel

Paper

Little red stones
that burn all night,
or coal

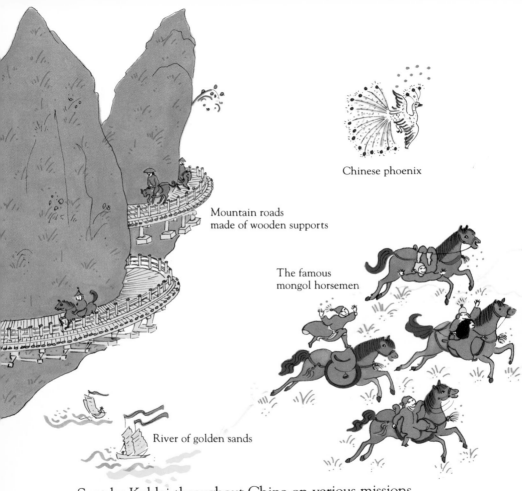

Chinese phoenix

Mountain roads
made of wooden supports

The famous
mongol horsemen

River of golden sands

Sent by Kublai throughout China on various missions,
Marco saw many more wonders.

Dragon dance
for new year

Unicorn

Pekinese

Panda

Tattooed man

Devil dancers

Acrobats and
street entertainers

Marco captured elephants for Kublai in one battle

and introduced Italian slings in another.

As a reward, the emperor sent Marco in the
care of master sailors down the Yangtze River

Deep and treacherous waters

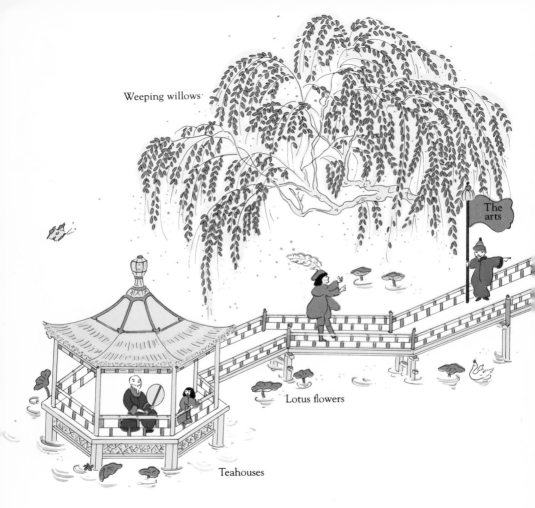

Weeping willows

The arts

Lotus flowers

Teahouses

and made him governor of Kinsai,

Poetry

Dance

Painting

Opera

Music

Puppets

the most civilized city in the world.

Kublai asked Marco to escort Princess Cocachin to Persia
to marry Argun Khan.

They set out from Zayton in remarkable Chinese ships with watertight compartments.

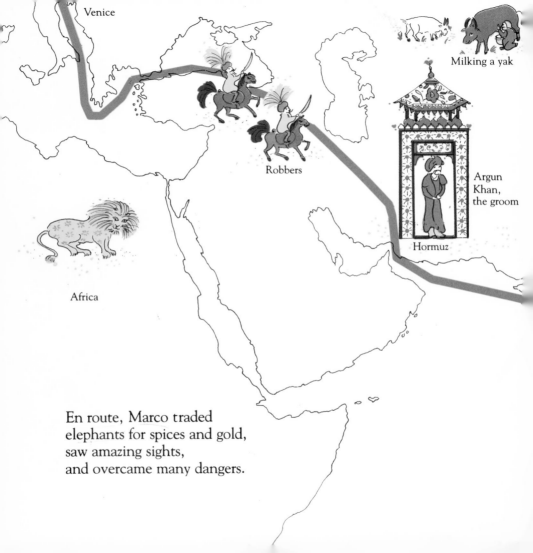

Venice

Milking a yak

Robbers

Argun
Khan,
the groom

Hormuz

Africa

En route, Marco traded
elephants for spices and gold,
saw amazing sights,
and overcame many dangers.

Mongolia

Yurts

Five hundred wives of
an Indian prince

Dancing elephants

India

Rubies

Ceylon

Fishermen diving
for pearls

Burma

High seas and
dangerous waters

Man-eating,
savage Sumatra

Zayton

Strange
birds

Borneo

Gold

In Persia the Argun Khan had died, so the princess married his son.

Marco began the journey home but was robbed on the way.

Poorer in goods but rich in experience,
Marco returned to Venice
after twenty-four years, at the age of forty-one.

The End

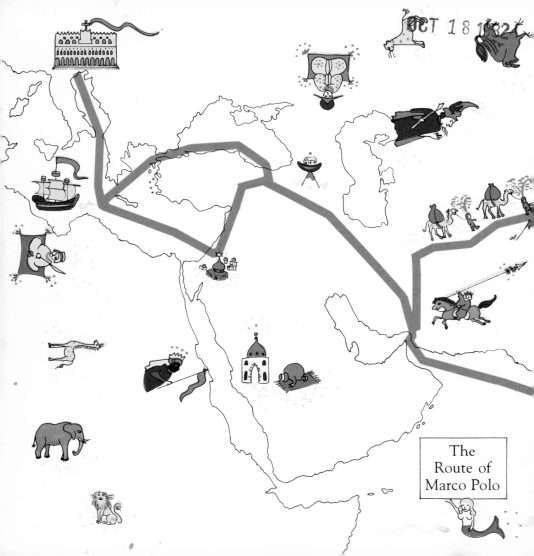

The
Route of
Marco Polo